Published in 2014 by Helen Exley® Gifts in Great Britain.
Design, selection and arrangement © Helen Exley Creative Ltd 2014
Illustrated by Juliette Clarke © Helen Exley Creative Ltd 2014

The moral right of the author has been asserted.

12 11 10 9 8 7 6 5 4 3 2 1

ISBN 978-1-84634-730-6

Helen Exley Gifts
16 Chalk Hill, Watford, Herts WD19 4BG, UK.
www.helenexley.com

You can follow us on and

A gem of a
Daughter

ILLUSTRATED BY JULIETTE CLARKE

HELEN EXLEY® GIFTS

ABOUT THIS BOOK

Here, in this treasure of a book,
are hundreds of the very best words
about daughters – words about the joy
they bring and the pride they inspire.
This book is a celebration
of their kindness and friendship,
and the many ways in which
they enrich our lives.

Helen Exley Gifts give pleasure to
millions of people every year,
which is why Helen and her team
take such pains to make these little books
such little jewels.
So enjoy this special gift!

CHAPTER 1

YOU BRING HAPPINESS, SMILES AND SERENITY

I love your smiles,
I see them everywhere.
No matter where I am,
no matter where
you are, your smiles will
always stay with me.

SIÂN E. MORGAN, B.1973

A tiny daughter
gives parents
a life in a climate of
perpetual wonder.

PIERRE DOUCET

Sometimes, as you lay peacefully
sleeping in your crib,
I would gently take your tiny hand
in mine just to share your peace
and serenity.

LINDA MACFARLANE B.1953

A Child of Happiness
always seems like an old
soul living in a new body,
and her face is very serious
until she smiles,
and then the sun lights
up the world...

ANNE CAMERON,
FROM "DAUGHTERS
OF COPPER WOMAN"

*Her laugh
is as wide and
wise as winter.
There is nothing filmy
nor flimsy about her.
She feeds as firmly
as the heart
mills blood...*

JENNIFER MAIDEN,
FROM "THE WINTER BABY"

WHAT FEELING IS
SO NICE AS A CHILD'S HAND
IN YOURS? SO SMALL,
SO SOFT AND WARM,
LIKE A KITTEN HUDDLING
IN THE SHELTER
OF YOUR CLASP.

MARJORIE HOLMES

Emily is wonderful:
she's like the sun,
she comes out
and everyone starts
feeling warmer.

JILLY COOPER, B.1937, FROM
THE "DAILY MAIL", APRIL 6, 1996

When I am feeling
weary and all the world
is dreary with thin
incessant rain, I think
about my daughter,
her brightness and her
laughter, and life comes
right again.

PAM BROWN, B.1928

A daughter is the...
object of a pleasure
something like
the love between the
angels to her father.

RICHARD STEELE
(1672-1729)

Parents droop a little
sometimes –
but then they think of
their daughters –
their verve and
their good-heartedness,
their achievements...
And feel much better.

PAM BROWN, B.1928

CHAPTER 2
ABSOLUTE LOVE

FROM THE INSTANT
I SAW HER...
I LOVED HER
WITH AN INTENSITY
THAT LIFE HAD
NOT PREPARED
ME FOR.

SUSAN CHEEVER

I AM A FOOL
FOR HER LOVE.

NICHOLAS LAZARD

*O*ur daughter, meanwhile,
was fast asleep herself,
one little hand showing
above the bedclothes.
Clenched in it was my heart.

HUGO WILLIAMS, B.1942

It was Tilly who first roused
in me the fiercest, deepest
feeling of love I have ever
experienced…
Before she was born,
I was unfulfilled, an
emotionally smaller person.
She brought about this new
growth in me…

FRASER HARRISON

She climbed into
my lap and curled into
the crook of my left arm…
I could kiss the top of
her head. And I could have
no doubt that this was one
of the sweetest moments
of my life.

DENNIS BYRD

I have never had
any person in my life
I love as much as
my daughter.
And I would trade
nothing for her.

FRED DEAN

W<small>HEN</small> I <small>LOOK</small>
<small>INTO YOUR EYES</small>
I <small>FEEL MINE</small>
<small>SHINE WITH LOVE.</small>

LINDA MACFARLANE, B.1953

Before you were conceived
I wanted you
Before you were born
I loved you
Before you were here an hour
I would die for you
This is the miracle of life.

MAUREEN HAWKINS

*F*or my sake, pray
cherish the person whom
*I love above all others
in the world.*

MME. DE SEVIGNE
(1626-1696)
IN A LETTER TO HER DAUGHTER

Arthur always had his arms around [his daughter] Camera. When he talked about her, his face would light up like stars in the sky. He showed more feeling for his daughter than I had seen him show his whole life.

HORACE ASHE,
UNCLE OF ARTHUR ASHE

Thou, straggler into
loving arms,
Young climber-up
of knees,
When I forget
thy thousand ways
Then life and
all shall cease.

MARY LAMB (1775-1834)

I didn't need
to seek out love,
I got more
than my share
of that from
my daughter.

MARSHA HUNT, B.1946,
FROM "REAL LIFE"

He is totally transformed
by his first daughter.
There is a gentleness about
him that even love
never discovered. He holds her...
like thinnest glass.
He wonders at this new
and lovely life...

PAM BROWN, B.1928

I wish that (if ever she sees this)
I could give my eldest daughter,
Marianne the slightest idea of
the love and the hope that is bound
up in her. The love which passeth
every earthly love...

ELIZABETH GASKELL (1810-1865),
FROM "MY DIARY"

No man can possibly know
what life means, what the world
means, what anything means,
until he has a child and loves it.
And then the whole universe changes
and nothing will ever again seem
exactly as it seemed before.

LAFCADIO HEARN

CHAPTER 3

WHEN YOU CAME INTO MY LIFE

...as the doctor shoved
cotton wool up your flat nose
and swabbed your eyes
and cleaned your bum
I forgot completely all my life
and love and watched you
like a pool of growing light
and whispered to myself
"She's come! She's come!"

BRIAN JONES

No one understands
how someone so little
can so change their world –
until they hold their baby
in their arms.

PAM BROWN, B.1928

I'LL NEVER FORGET
THE FIRST TIME
I SAW YOU. YOU WERE WET,
STICKY, WRINKLY AND
SCREAMING YOUR HEAD OFF.
THE MOST PERFECT,
BEAUTIFUL SIGHT
I HAD EVER SEEN.

STUART MACFARLANE, B.1953

During the first weeks,
I used to lie long hours
with the baby in my arms,
watching her sleep;
sometimes catching a gaze
from her eyes:
feeling very near the edge,
the mystery,
perhaps the knowledge
of life.

ISADORA DUNCAN (1878-1927)

The baby has learned to smile, and her smiles burst forth like holiday sparklers, lighting our hearts... At what are we smiling? We don't know, and we don't care. We are communicating with one another in happiness...

JOAN LOWERY NIXON

Then someone placed
her in my arms.
She looked up at me…
Her eyes melted through me,
forging a connection
in me with their soft heat.
I felt her love power stir
in my heart.

SHIRLEY MACLAINE, B.1934

Suddenly she
was here.
And I was no
longer pregnant,
I was a mother.
I never believed
in miracles before.

ELLEN GREENE

She held my attention
like a fiery constellation.
Her eyes bewitched me.
Her first smile caused me and
Jon to waltz around the room
with the baby between us.
We were besotted with her,
the first parents in history.

ERICA JONG, B.1942
FROM "FEAR OF FIFTY"

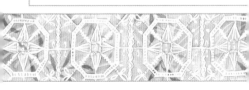

I loved you the very first second that I saw your face. But how could I begin to suspect the astonishments held in the bundle of blanket? You are my delight — my never-ending source of amazement!

PAMELA DUGDALE

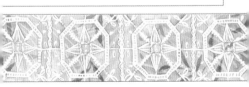

Chapter 4

Daughters make all things new

Your first butterfly.
Your first rainbow.
Your first dinosaur.
Thank you
for the chance
to rediscover
the world.

PAMELA DUGDALE

A daughter
is a new beginning.

PAM BROWN, B.1928

Thank you for
reminding me of
summer nights, romance
and the taste of
peanut butter.

CHARLOTTE GRAY, B.1937

A DAUGHTER REMINDS
YOU OF ALL THE THINGS
YOU HAD FORGOTTEN
ABOUT BEING YOUNG.
GOOD AND BAD.

MAEVE O'REILLY

Thank you for giving me back Pooh Bear and Ratty and Curdie and Milly-Molly-Mandy. Thank you for reminding me of stars and fallen leaves, winter beaches, summer woods. Thank you for tadpoles and spiders named Alfred.

PAM BROWN, B.1928

So often you
put your hand
in mine
or we link arms
and step out in
the world together,
just spellbound
in amazement.

SIÂN E. MORGAN, B.1973

*Thank you for believing
my birthday cakes
were magical, my paintings
amazing, my stories
the best in the world.
Children allow grown-ups
to relive enchantment.*

PAM BROWN, B.1928

I never know
what the day will bring.
That's the beauty
of having a daughter.

SIÂN E. MORGAN, B.1973

CHAPTER 5

WRAPPED AROUND YOUR LITTLE FINGER

Wrapped round her little finger?!
Not at all!!
I wanted to buy her all those teddies, dolls, books...

STUART MACFARLANE, B.1953

How can one say
no to a child?
How can one be
anything but a slave
to one's own flesh
and blood?

HENRY MILLER
(1891-1980)

WITH A CHEEKY GURGLE AND A PLAYFUL CHUCKLE YOU CAPTURED EVERYONE'S HEART.

STUART AND LINDA MACFARLANE

Dad has long
and earnest conversations
with his baby daughter.
He tells her she is noisy,
undisciplined and
manipulative…
And the baby smiles
complacently.
She has him exactly
where she wants him.

PAM BROWN, B.1928

Violet Elizabeth
dried her tears.
She saw that they
were useless
and she did not
believe in wasting
her effects. "All right,"
she said calmly,
"I'll thcream then,

I'll thcream,
an' thcream,
an'thcream till
I'm thick."

RICHMAL CROMPTON
(1890-1969)

The whisper
of a baby girl
can be heard
further than
the roar of a lion.

ARAB PROVERB

*O*ne of the ironies of being
a parent is that you have your
children a limited number of years,
and you seldom see them.
You may seldom hear from them.
But the power a child
has over you lasts a lifetime.

BETTE DAVIS (1908-1989)

I know I have
my father wrapped around
my little finger;
but he has me wrapped
around his.

HOLLY HESTON, DAUGHTER
OF CHARLTON HESTON

Chapter 6

Uniquely
Beautifully
You

Never forget
– you're not
just special to me.
You're special.
And that's that.

PAM BROWN, B.1928

I think of you
as my best investment,
my best work,
my best achievement,
the very best
thing I ever did.

SIÂN E. MORGAN, B.1973

Small child. Clear crystal.
Bright and clear.
Faceted as none before you.
Catching the light
from every lovely thing
and turning it to rainbow.
Reflecting beauty back
into the world.
Making all things new.

PAMELA DUGDALE

My daughter
is now six years old.
This, to me,
is much more a miracle
than having three books
on the bestseller list
at the same time.

MICHAEL CRICHTON

Having children
is like planting
seeds from an
unmarked packet.
You vaguely believe
that you are going
to get daisies.

Instead, you get
orchids, roses,
morning glories,
sunflowers…
But all beautiful.
Like you.

PAM BROWN, B.1928

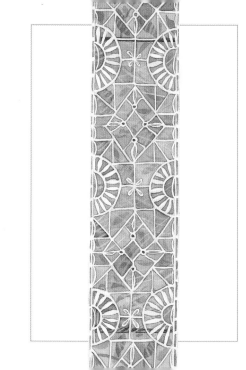

My child
is a Phenomenon,
really the most
wonderful
Natural Production
I ever beheld...

LADY HOLLAND

*I have a beautiful daughter,
golden like a flower,
my beloved Cleïs, for her,
in her place, I would not
accept the whole of Lydia...*

SAPPHO, C.650 B.C.

In the lottery of my life,
my daughter is the six
numbers – and the bonus.

AUTHOR UNKNOWN, FROM
"COSMOPOLITAN", MARCH 1997

Did I want a frilly
daughter or a chunky,
cheerful child?
Did I want her to be
an administrator?
Or caring? Or both?

As it was, I didn't get any of my dreams. I got a totally unique, totally puzzling, unpredictable, delightful you.

PAM BROWN, B.1928

Little Girl
My Stringbean,
My Lovely
Woman.

ANNE SEXTON
(1928-1974)

I'm proud of all
your achievements. I'm proud
of your looks and your
intelligence — which some
far distant ancestor
handed down. But I'm most
proud of your being just you.

PAM BROWN, B.1928

Chapter 7

Expense, trouble, moods and worry

You stormed into
our lives like a tornado.
You toddled over all
our plans. You screamed
through our best-loved
movies. You threw up
on everything. You made
our lives wonderful.

STUART AND LINDA MACFARLANE

A tiny daughter seems
like a dolly to dress –
but dolls do not sick, poo,
dribble – or apply liberal
quantities of paint and mud.
Satins and laces don't
last long on this living doll.

PAM BROWN, B.1928

One word of command from me
is obeyed by millions... but
I cannot get my three daughters,
Pamela, Felicity and Joan,
to come down
to breakfast on time.

VISCOUNT ARCHIBALD WAVELL
(1883-1950)

A *tiny, new,*
baby daughter
is a giant phone bill
waiting to happen.

STUART AND LINDA
MACFARLANE

They say,
"a daughter is worth
her weight in gold,"
they don't tell you
that she will cost you
that amount
every month.

STUART AND LINDA
MACFARLANE

I have so many anxieties
about her growing up…
I hope there is a world for her
to grow up in. I watch the
news and think, "they're going
to blow up the world, just when
I've got this little peach here."

MERYL STREEP, B.1949

*So many scary moments
have been and gone. Something
upsetting on TV, illnesses, bullying
or broken hearts.
And in those moments...
absolutely nothing in the world
could compare to your
well-being, your health, your safety.*

SIÂN E. MORGAN, B.1973

My dear daughter,
be very good.
Do not bump yourself...
Do not play with scissors
or cats. Do not forget
your dad. Sleep when
your mother wishes it.
Love us both.
Try to know how
we love you...

LETTER BY
RICHARD HARDING DAVIS

Rather suspiciously
the words
"I didn't..."
were often uttered
before the question
was ever asked.

GIOVANNI ANDRETTI

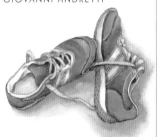

Wasn't it strange
that when she started
to choose her own
clothes the shopping
bill doubled?

STUART AND LINDA MACFARLANE

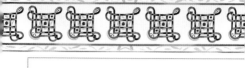

A daughter's clothes
can be very silly
indeed. As silly as yours
were at the same age,
just differently silly.

PAM BROWN, B.1928

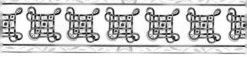

THE QUICKEST WAY
TO GET YOUR CHILDREN'S
ATTENTION
IS TO SIT DOWN AND LOOK
COMFORTABLE.

AUTHOR UNKNOWN

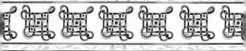

The ancient Greek
who wrote of Medusa
the Gorgon,
and her ability to turn men
to stone simply by looking
at them, had probably just
escaped from a confrontation
with his daughter.

CHRISTINE HARRIS

If a man smiles at home
somebody is sure to ask
him for money.

WILLIAM FEATHER

There was a little girl
Who had a little curl
Right in the middle
of her forehead,
And when she was good
She was very, very good
But when she was bad
she was horrid.

HENRY WADSWORTH LONGFELLOW

I love you even for
those slammed doors…
for taking my clothes
without asking, late nights
with no call…
They've all been forgiven.

SIÂN E. MORGAN, B.1973

A daughter is the person
to whom all that stuff
that has been twenty years
in the attic belongs.

PAM BROWN, B.1928

Things change so fast...
Whatever she does is going
to look far-out to me.
I hope I'll either like it or
keep my mouth shut.

GRACE SLICK,
ABOUT HER INFANT DAUGHTER

A daughter is
the person you thought
you would stop
worrying about when
she hit twenty-one.
But who is still worrying
you silly at forty-five.

PAM BROWN, B.1928

Chapter 8

All the different yous

I love all
the different yous…
The adorable wicked
little girl, the developing
teenage girl
(with a mind of her own!),
the accomplished
young woman.

SIÂN E. MORGAN, B.1973

I think daughters have
all been here before
– they change from little
children to wise old
women almost overnight
when their families are
confronted by hard times.

PAM BROWN, B.1928

From crawling to driving in an instance. Time disappeared so quickly. Yet, I am blessed to have shared it with you.

STUART MACFARLANE, B.1953

I WATCH AS YOU HAVE
DISCOVERED YOURSELF
AND WHAT YOU CAN DO,
AS YOU BECOME WHAT
YOU ARE TRULY
CAPABLE OF.

SIÂN E. MORGAN,
B.1973

...to see you all developing
from tiny helpless babies...
to see your minds changing
with your years and to remember
that some day you will be grown...
women. It is overwhelming.

MRS. COLBERT,
FROM "A LETTER TO HER DAUGHTER
JANE", C.1930

I keep an album of photographs
of you – as if I could hold on to
all the different yous – the baby,
the school-girl, the teenager.
But they don't really matter.
…Because you are all of them
– and every time I see you I think
"This is the best time."

PAM BROWN, B.1928

CHAPTER 9
TEENAGER!

There comes a moment
in every parent's life
when they feel it would have
been better to have bred
Spaniels, or Siamese cats...
Nature has mercifully
ensured, however,
that teenage girls grow
bearable and wise at exactly
the moment they were due
to be thrown out.

PAM BROWN, B.1928

Teenage girls!
If the phone's
not engaged
the bathroom is.

AMANDA BELL

When you were twelve we agreed that as you were all grown up you should tidy your own room. That was seven years ago and you've still not got around to it.

STUART AND LINDA MACFARLANE

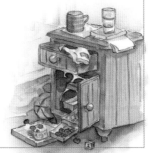

[Daughters] are inclined to… attach themselves to strange groups and causes. And stranger boyfriends. To veer between ecstasy

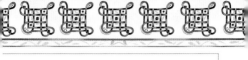

and misery. To drop
bombshells. They are
trying lives on for size.
The daughter you know
and love is still there.

PAM BROWN, B.1928

I HAVE FOUND THE BEST
WAY TO GIVE ADVICE
TO YOUR CHILDREN IS TO
FIND OUT WHAT THEY WANT
AND THEN ADVISE THEM
TO DO IT.

HARRY S. TRUMAN
(1884-1972)

There's nothing wrong
with teenagers that
reasoning with them
won't aggravate.

AUTHOR UNKNOWN

Undoubtedly, the first man who ever tore a telephone book in half had a teen-aged daughter.

JOAN I. WELSH

A daughter is
an awful reminder
of the way
you behaved
at fourteen.

PAM BROWN, B.1928

All parents
worry about
all daughters
at all times.
The best cure
is to hear
them laughing.

PAM BROWN, B.1928

*W*hen our phone rings,
it's always for my daughter.
When it isn't ringing,
it's because she's talking on it.
Sometimes when she's on
our phone, the neighbors will
come over and tell her she's
wanted on their phone.

ART FRANK

Chapter 10

Precious
memories

I love all those keepsakes that have accumulated over the years. Each one tells a different story.

SIÂN E. MORGAN, B.1973

Your first swan. Your first day by the sea. Your first walk through a field of spring flowers. The first time you heard and loved Chopin. In sharing your childhood discoveries, I have relived my own.

MARION C. GARRETTY (1917-2005)

I love to look at all those photos of you. How they make me laugh when I rediscover them again. No hair, baby hair, bright red hair! No clothes, baby gros, dressing up clothes, clothes that make me hold my breath!

SIÂN E. MORGAN, B.1973

We have
filled the house
with a lifetime
of laughter
crammed with
so many
memories.

SIÂN E. MORGAN, B.1973

I wonder if you remember how we
loved long days in the country?...
How we all put on our bright gloves
and went crunching into the snow?...
Your tiny boots? I remember.
I always will.

HELEN THOMSON

Thank you for remembering my stories, loving my made-up games in the backyard and saying all your friends loved the birthday parties I over-organised!

LYNN MCLEAN

We played, we sang,
we danced wildly.
And we wandered quietly
by the sea. I will always
remember these days
in summer – they're in
my very being.

HELEN THOMSON

CHAPTER 11
THANK YOU FOR YOUR KINDNESS

Thanks for all
the cards – hand drawn
or by Renoir. For all the
parcels – knobbly or
beribboned.
For all the hurried kisses –
smelling of chocolate
or Chanel.
For remembering.

PAM BROWN, B.1928

*Thank you for wilting
dandelions, for
twigs of lamb's-tails,
for wet pebbles,
for fluff-covered toffees,
for sticky kisses.
Thank you for
loving me.*

PAMELA DUGDALE

I might protest at first,
but secretly I'm glad you
insist I put my feet up whilst
I have a cup of tea.

SIÂN E. MORGAN, B.1973

Sometimes when I'm feeling
particularly useless you give me
sound advice — which I once
gave you... Thanks for keeping
an eye on me, love.

PAMELA DUGDALE

She phones me
regularly to keep tabs
on me. When I'm
not tranquil, she will
try to steady me.
My periods of loneliness,
she reassures me.
What a marvellous
daughter she is!

ROMILDA VILLANI,
FROM "SOPHIA: LIVING AND LOVING"

Some daughters give
Cartier watches and
Cointreau. Some daughters
send shrubs, sweaters
and home-made jam.
The thing is – daughters
know exactly what
one needs.

PAMELA DUGDALE

Thirty-four years of happy smiles, of loving looks and gentle words, of generous deeds. Thirty-four years, a flower, a palm, a star, a faultless child, a perfect woman, wife, and mother.

ROBERT G. INGERSOLL (1833-1899), IN A BIRTHDAY NOTE TO HIS DAUGHTER EVA

CHAPTER 12
TIMES WHEN WE ARE APART

A child enters your
home and makes so much
noise for twenty years
you can hardly stand it
– then departs, leaving the
house so silent you think
you will go mad.

DR. J. A. HOLMES

Even if you're
not here,
those memories
of you dance
around me,
wherever I go.

SIÂN E. MORGAN, B.1973

*I*n the dark hours
before dawn, *I* put on the lamp
and read your last letter,
full of news, full of plans
and adventures, opinions
and excitements. And the past
falls into perspective.

PAM BROWN, B.1928

...all you do – despite your freedom – must affect me too. And so when we're apart I will always long for news from you.

MAYA PATEL, B.1943

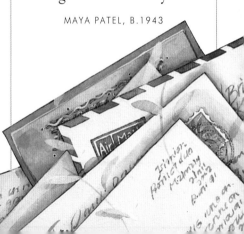

IT WILL BE GONE
BEFORE YOU KNOW IT.
THE FINGERPRINTS ON
THE WALL APPEAR
HIGHER AND HIGHER.
THEN SUDDENLY THEY
DISAPPEAR.

DOROTHY EVSLIN

IT'S FAR EASIER, MY LOVE,
TO SEE YOUR WORTH NOW
THE BATHROOM IS NO LONGER
DENSE WITH TALCUM SMOG
AND SOGGY WITH TOWELS…
AND I CAN CALL A PAIR OF SHOES
MY OWN. I DO LOVE YOU.
EVEN MORE NOW!

CHARLOTTE GRAY, B.1937

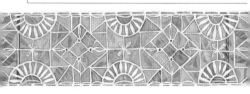

There is nothing, absolutely nothing that can cheer up a dismal evening of TV repeats and yesterday's leftovers more successfully than a phone call from a daughter.

PAM BROWN, B.1928

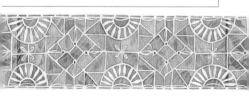

Our letters
have been a strong
life-line stretched
half way around
the world:
to me they
are a continuous
message of love
and dependence...

IVY SPENDER

Chapter 13
Holding
each
other up

*...you can do anything
you put your mind to...
Mom and Dad will give
you all the support, love,
advice, and help you need
to reach your goal.*

SABRINA, TO HER DAUGHTERS

It was this deep, loving understanding as long as she lived that more than anything else helped and sustained me on my way to success.

MAE WEST (1892-1980)

There are things I cannot stick together, or heal with a hug... I wish I had some magic that could make such things come right. All I can do is be here. Always.

PAM BROWN, B.1928

*T*he most sophisticated,
capable, successful daughter howls
for her parents in a crisis.
The most modern and socially
involved mother or father
will drop everything to rush
to a daughter in trouble.

JANET M. BRIDGES

You have to
fight your own battles,
love. But I'm here
in your corner with
the bucket and sponge.

PAM BROWN, B.1928

In those saddest moments,
I am reminded that you're not
completely invincible.
Not just yet. And secretly
I'm glad that you sometimes,
just sometimes, still need me.

SIÂN E. MORGAN, B.1973

*A*s we move off into
the future, two separate women
each struggling to complete
herself, I know that we will
reach out to each other.
In my strength I can be a tree
for you to lean against.

RITA FREEMAN

If there is anything
in my life that can be
of value to you,
I want you to have it;
if I can save you a stumble
or a single false step,
I want to do it.

FLORENCE WENDEROTH SAUNDERS

My love will
be with you
When life's woes
weigh you down.

My love will
be with you

When life is fearful.
My love will
be with you
Today and forever.

STUART MACFARLANE, B.1953

CHAPTER 14

MY DAUGHTER MY FRIEND

The best
thing you have
given me is your
friendship.

PAM BROWN, B.1928

I'm so thankful to God
that I have one healthy,
gorgeous, beautiful child.
I even love her bones.
We are so close. She is my
very best friend.

FAITH BROWN

We've had some
fights, you and I.
The sort that only we
could have and still be
friends. (I like it most
when we end up laughing!)

SIÂN E. MORGAN, B.1973

Thank you for showing me, when I thought my mothering days were over, that the best days between us are only just beginning.

PAM BROWN, B.1928

...she is a wise, giving, deeply loving daughter and friend. The chasm that existed between us is now, thankfully, a meadowland of conversation and love.

DEBBIE REYNOLDS, B.1932

No one else could be so easily forgiven for dropping everything across chairs, beds and floors. No one but you.

Even if we don't always see eye to eye, it always works out in the end. I could never stay cross with you for long.

SIÂN E. MORGAN, B.1973

It was a joy to see you grow
— but a sadness too — for you
found your independence and no
longer needed me. But now I see
that the years have given more
than they have taken — and I
celebrate my daughter and
my friend.

PAM BROWN, B.1928

Chapter 15
Be your own true self

My mother
raised me,
and then
freed me.

MAYA ANGELOU, B.1928

May you never
cease to search
and challenge.
May you discover
what you want
to do – and
do it well.

PAM BROWN, B.1928

*...take all the gifts
that you were born
with and make
of them marvels
of beauty and ingenuity
and astonishment.*

CHARLOTTE GRAY, B.1937

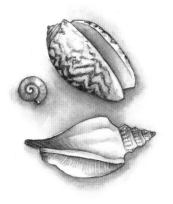

I wrapped you
in protection, yet each
time telling myself "teach
her to clad herself in
armor and be brave."
I must remember to love
her enough to let her fall.

DONNA GREEN

She had her own life to lead, her own destiny to accomplish; she just came past me to this earth. My job was to get her to adulthood and then push her off.

KATHARINE TREVELYAN

*M*y mother's best advice
to me was: "Whatever you
decide to do in life, be sure
that the joy of doing it does
not depend upon the applause
of others, because in the long
run we are, all of us, alone."

ALI MACGRAW

My dream… is that they will grow into beautiful young women who love themselves and therefore don't need to be validated by anyone else…

JAYNE KENNEDY OVERTON,
ABOUT HER DAUGHTERS

What I wanted
most for my daughter
was that she be able
to soar confidently
in her own sky,
wherever that
might be…

HELEN CLAES

Risk! Risk anything!
Care no more for
the opinion of others,
for those voices.
Do the hardest thing
on earth for you.
Act for yourself.

KATHERINE MANSFIELD (1888-1923)

IN A WORLD WHERE
IT IS NECESSARY TO
SUCCEED, PERHAPS ONLY
WE WOMEN KNOW
MORE DEEPLY THAT
SUCCESS CAN BE A QUIET
AND HIDDEN THING.

PAM BROWN, B.1928

*M*y dream for Ashley
and Alexandra is to raise them
to be all they can be...
human beings who not only
find, but aren't afraid to go
after, whatever it is
that makes them happy in life.

VANESSA BELL CALLOWAY

...I dream I could give you all the places I couldn't take you – Florence and Venice and Rome, Paris and Prague... But you might not want them. I wish you your own places, your own adventures...

PAM BROWN, B.1928

Never grow
a wishbone,
daughter, where
your backbone
ought to be.

CLEMENTINE PADDLEFORD

My mother taught
me to walk proud
and tall "as if the
world was mine".

SOPHIA LOREN, B.1934

Chapter 16
My wishes
for you

I wish you happy
and secure and
comfortable and wise.
But not yet. Get the
adventures in first.

PAM BROWN, B.1928

*...to claim your life
and fight like hell for
your right to be;
and the best gift that
I could ever give to you
was to say "yes" to your
dreams that were not
my own.*

MARGARET SLOAN-HUNTER,
FROM "PASSING"

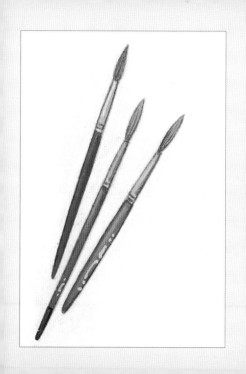

You are our bright star. You light our lives. I wish you discoveries and marvels. I wish you success that has no sting. I wish you joy and peace and warm contentment. And always, always, love.

PAM BROWN, B.1928

Love, peace and an
enquiring mind.
That's what I wish for you...
Together with the ability
to stand in other people's
shoes. And to laugh
at yourself.

JONATHON A. HUGHES

I wish you the beauty
of silence, the glory
of sunlight, the mystery
of darkness...
the power of water,
the sweetness of air,

the quiet strength
of earth, the love that
lies at the very root
of things. I wish you the
wonder of living.

PAM BROWN, B.1928

I wish I could save
you from anxiety
and sorrow.
But then – how pink
and fluffy and
monotonous

your life would be!
So I wish for you
courage and clear
thinking, hope and a
happy heart.
This year – and always.

PAMELA DUGDALE

Dear. I hope
that when you are
very, very old you
can look back and say,
"Heavens. That was
a lovely life."

PAM BROWN, B.1928

My prayer is that you
will learn those characteristics
that are worthy of possessing:
love, servanthood, honesty,
sincerity… I can only hope
that I can be an example
to you.

AMY, FROM LETTERS
TO OUR DAUGHTERS

*I wish you
a daughter
just like you.*

PAM BROWN, B.1928

Chapter 17

A bond
so strong

...you are,
above everything,
the heartbeat
of my life.

*S*he holds out
her hand to air,
Sea, sky, wind, sun,
movement, stillness.
And wants to hold
them all. My finger
is her earth connection,
me, and earth.

JENNIFER ARMITAGE,
FROM "TO OUR DAUGHTER"

My love for her
and my hate
for her are so
bafflingly intertwined
that I can hardly

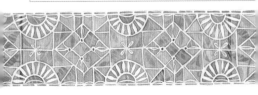

see her. I never know
who is who. She is
me and I am she
and we're all together.

ERICA JONG, B.1942

When you are a father, and you hear your children's voices, you will feel that those little ones are akin to every drop in your veins...

HONORÉ DE BALZAC (1799-1850), FROM "LE PÈRE GORIOT"

Whatever happens...
our lives are
stitched together
by a thread of gold
that cannot change,

whatever changes come.

PAM BROWN, B.1928

Romance fails us – and so do friendships – but the relationship – of Mother and Child – remains indelible and indestructible – the strongest bond upon this earth.

THEODOR REIK

You have my love – the love that links us. Take it with you into the world that I will never know.

PAM BROWN, B.1928

WHAT IS A
HELEN EXLEY GIFT BOOK?

Helen Exley Gift books cover
the most powerful of all human
relationships: the bonds within families
and between friends,
and the theme of personal values.
No expense is spared in making sure
that each book is as meaningful a gift
as it is possible to create: good to give,
good to receive.
You have the result in your hands.
If you have loved it – tell others!
There is no power on earth like
the word-of-mouth recommendation
of friends!